SUCCESS IN

Key Stage 3 Shakespeare

G000097688

Scene-specific preparation for the 2007 national test

Much Ado About Nothing

**MICHAEL JONES
KEVIN DYKE
and GEORGHIA ELLINAS**

Heinemann
From Harcourt

Introduction

Success in Key Stage 3 Shakespeare: **Much Ado About Nothing** is designed to build on your teaching of the play as a whole and help you to improve the performance of all your students in the Key Stage 3 Shakespeare test. Together the *Success in Key Stage 3 Shakespeare:* **Much Ado About Nothing** Student's Revision Book and Teacher's Notes provide a revision schedule and 14 lessons, ensuring that students engage with and revise character, theme, language and performance in the context of the set extracts. Once you have worked through the activities with your students, they will have explored the set scenes according to the four key areas of test questioning and learnt to support their points with quotations from the set extracts.

The Teacher's Notes are available at www.heinemann.co.uk/literature. They include:

- a scheme of work for 14 revision lessons with lesson plans showing how the summary activities can be used to engage students and enhance understanding
- additional information to support the activities in the Student's Revision Book.

Using *Success in Key Stage 3 Shakespeare:* **Much Ado About Nothing** to revise for the Key Stage 3 tests, you can be secure in the knowledge that your students have been well prepared for the test and should feel confident and prepared to answer any question that may be asked.

Heinemann Educational Publishers
Halley Court, Jordan Hill, Oxford OX2 8EJ
Part of Harcourt Education

Heinemann is the registered trademark of Harcourt Education Limited

© Harcourt, 2006

First published 2006

10 09 08 07 06
10 9 8 7 6 5 4 3 2 1

British Library Cataloguing in Publication Data is available
from the British Library on request.

10-digit ISBN: 0 435 99721 1
13-digit ISBN: 978 0 435997 21 2

Designed by GD Associates
Typeset by Tek-Art

Original illustrations © Harcourt Education Limited, 2006
Illustrated by Andy Morris
Printed in the UK by Ashford Colour Press

Cover photo: © Alamy

Success in Key Stage 3 Shakespeare: *Much Ado About Nothing*

Contents

Climax of feud.
- fearsome woman

how she hurts Benedict

The story of *Much Ado About Nothing*

1 Leonato, with his daughter Hero and niece Beatrice, wait to meet Don Pedro, Prince of Arragon, and his nobles. Beatrice makes comments at the expense of one of the expected noblemen – Benedick – with whom she has a war of wit.

2 Don Pedro, Prince of Arragon, returns victorious from war, accompanied by Claudio & Benedick, both successful soldiers. The war was against Don Pedro's own brother, Don John.

3 Benedick is notorious for his rude remarks about women. He makes fun of Claudio for falling in love with Hero. Don Pedro, by contrast, agrees to woo Hero on Claudio's behalf, and does so.

4 Don John, brother of Don Pedro, hates himself and the world. He takes pleasure in the idea of causing trouble to Don Pedro's favourite, Claudio.

5 Beatrice enjoys having fun at a masked ball by describing Benedick rudely, when (supposedly) neither knows who the other one is.

6 Claudio has been feeling jealous of Don Pedro. However having wooed Hero on behalf of Claudio, Don Pedro gains Leonato's consent and then hands over to Claudio his 'jewel' Hero. To occupy the time before the wedding, Don Pedro intends to 'bring Signor Benedick and Lady Beatrice into a mountain of affection.'

7 Don John's servant Borachio suggests a way of ruining the marriage by making it appear that Hero is unfaithful. His lover, Margaret, will call to him from a window so that the watchers (Claudio and Don Pedro) will mistake her for Hero.

8 Knowing that Benedick can overhear them, the Prince, Claudio and Leonato speak of Beatrice's love for Benedick. They convince him that she does indeed 'dote' on him.

9 Hero and her gentlewomen speak of Benedick's love for Beatrice, knowing that she can overhear them.

10 Don John persuades Claudio & Don Pedro to join him to witness what he claims will be Hero's betrayal.

11 Claudio shames Hero at the moment when he was to marry her, and does so with maximum cruelty.

12 Friar Francis suggests that they change attitudes and the atmosphere by putting out news that Hero has died.

Meanwhile, the local watch, although they are figures of fun, accidentally overhear and arrest Don John's villains, Conrade and Borachio.

13 Benedick promises Beatrice that he will challenge Claudio to defend Hero's honour.

14 Don John's plot is exposed by his servants who have been arrested by the Watch under Constable Dogberry.

15 Thinking that Hero is dead, Claudio has agreed to marry Leonato's niece. He and Don Pedro go to what they think is Hero's tomb, only to find that the woman is Hero herself, back from the dead.

16 Beatrice and Benedick acknowledge their love for each other, but in their own witty ways and to the amusement of everyone.

Set extracts

Extract 1: Act 1, Scene 1, lines 1 to 123

Performance

Leonato leads the group to show he is the most important person on the stage; the messenger should be just behind him, and Beatrice and Hero walk together with arms linked to show they are close friends

Outside Leonato's house.
Enter LEONATO (Governor of Messina), his daughter
HERO, *his niece* BEATRICE *and a* MESSENGER.

LEONATO
I learn in this letter that Don Pedro of Aragon comes this night to Messina.

MESSENGER
He is very near by this; he was not three leagues off when I left him.

Character

Leonato asks only about the gentlemen (important people) and not about soldiers who may have been killed; this shows how he is interested in people who have status or titles, like him

LEONATO
How many gentlemen have you lost in this action?   5

MESSENGER
But few of any sort, and none of name.

LEONATO
A victory is twice itself when the achiever brings home full numbers. I find here that Don Pedro hath bestowed much honour on a young Florentine called Claudio.

Performance

Leonato should point to a part in the letter and show it to the messenger to signal how he is impressed with Claudio's achievements

MESSENGER
Much deserved on his part, and equally remembered by   10
Don Pedro. He hath borne himself beyond the promise of his age, doing in the figure of a lamb the feats of a lion. He hath indeed better bettered expectation than you must expect of me to tell you how.

**Theme:
appearance and
reality**

People do not always behave like they look; Claudio looks young and playful, but is actually a fierce fighter

Theme: honour

Leonato points out that Claudio's reputation will make his uncle proud of him

LEONATO
He hath an uncle here in Messina will be very much   15
glad of it.

MESSENGER
I have already delivered him letters, and there appears much joy in him; even so much that joy could not show itself modest enough without a badge of bitterness.

Language

This is a happy time; the war has been won and the army is returning; by using the word 'joy' so many times, this emphasises how happy everyone is and creates a good atmosphere

LEONATO
Did he break out into tears?   20

MESSENGER
In great measure.

LEONATO
A kind overflow of kindness. There are no faces truer than those that are so washed. How much better is it to weep a joy than to joy at weeping!

Language

The prose style in this opening scene creates a relaxed and natural picture of society in Messina

Performance

Beatrice should tap the messenger on the shoulder so that he has to turn away from Leonato; he answers her question, then turns back to Leonato to show she is not as important

Character

Hero knows who Beatrice is talking about; this shows she understands her cousin

Performance

Beatrice should push out her stomach and rub it to show that she thinks Benedick is fat and greedy

Character

Beatrice refers back to her earlier joke about Benedick as a ladies' man

Character

Beatrice shows how clever she is by playing with the joke about Cupid

Language

The repetition of 'killed' adds a harsh note to Beatrice's joke about Benedick

Theme: honour

The messenger defends Benedick by telling Beatrice that Benedick has a reputation of being a good soldier, which is very important

BEATRICE
I pray you, is Signior Mountanto returned from the wars, 25
or no?

MESSENGER
I know none of that name, lady; there was none such in
the army of any sort.

LEONATO
What is he that you ask for, niece?

HERO
My cousin means Signior Benedick of Padua.   30

MESSENGER
O, he's returned, and as pleasant as ever he was.

BEATRICE
He set up his bills here in Messina, and challenged
Cupid at the flight; and my uncle's fool, reading the
challenge, subscribed for Cupid, and challenged him at
the bird-bolt. I pray you, how many hath he killed and   35
eaten in these wars? But how many hath he killed? For
indeed I promised to eat all of his killing.

LEONATO
Faith, niece, you tax Signior Benedick too much; but
he'll be meet with you, I doubt it not.

MESSENGER
He hath done good service, lady, in these wars.   40

BEATRICE
You had musty victual, and he hath holp to eat it. He is
a very valiant trencher-man; he hath an excellent
stomach.

MESSENGER
And a good soldier too, lady.

BEATRICE
And a good soldier to a lady. But what is he to a lord?   45

MESSENGER
A lord to a lord, a man to a man, stuffed with all
honourable virtues.

BEATRICE
It is so, indeed; he is no less than a stuffed man. But for the stuffing – well, we are all mortal.

LEONATO
You must not, sir, mistake my niece. There is a kind of   50
merry war betwixt Signior Benedick and her. They never meet but there's a skirmish of wit between them.

BEATRICE
Alas, he gets nothing by that. In our last conflict four of his five wits went halting off, and now is the whole man governed with one: so that if he have wit enough to   55
keep himself warm, let him bear it for a difference between himself and his horse; for it is all the wealth that he hath left, to be known a reasonable creature. Who is his companion now? He hath every month a new sworn brother.   60

MESSENGER
Is't possible?

BEATRICE
Very easily possible. He wears his faith but as the fashion of his hat: it ever changes with the next block.

MESSENGER
I see, lady, the gentleman is not in your books.

BEATRICE
No: an he were, I would burn my study. But, I pray you,   65
who is his companion? Is there no young squarer now that will make a voyage with him to the devil?

MESSENGER
He is most in the company of the right noble Claudio.

BEATRICE
O Lord, he will hang upon him like a disease. He is sooner caught than the pestilence, and the taker runs   70
presently mad. God help the noble Claudio! If he have caught the Benedick, it will cost him a thousand pound ere 'a be cured.

MESSENGER
I will hold friends with you, lady.

Theme
Battle of the sexes

Language
The use of 'he', 'his' and 'himself' means Beatrice does not have to mention Benedick by name; it has the effect of making him seem unimportant – which, of course, he is not

Language
Beatrice plays with the image of Benedick being in her good books to point out he will never achieve that because she would make sure she had no books at all

Performance
The messenger should hold up his hands as if surrendering to Beatrice and starts to back away from her, showing that he is frightened of her and she is too much for him to deal with

Language
'merry war' and 'skirmish' both suggest that the fight that Beatrice and Benedick are having is not serious; it is a light-hearted contest

Character
Beatrice is suggesting that Benedick is fickle and cannot be relied on; he changes his affection as often as he changes his hat

Language
This is a particularly savage insult as the use of the words 'pestilence' and 'disease' would be very unpleasant to an Elizabethan audience

Theme

Beatrice is a fierce female who dominates most men through her wit

BEATRICE
Do, good friend.   75

LEONATO
You will never run mad, niece.

BEATRICE
No, not till a hot January.

MESSENGER
Don Pedro is approached.

Enter DON PEDRO, CLAUDIO, BENEDICK, BALTHASAR *and* DON JOHN *the bastard (Don Pedro's half-brother).*

Performance

Don John should stand away from all the others and look very angry; this is to show he is not one of the group – he is an outsider

DON PEDRO
Good Signior Leonato, are you come to meet your trouble? The fashion of the world is to avoid cost, and   80
You encounter it.

Theme

Leonato's comments on 'the likeness of your Grace' reminds us of the difference between appearance and reality – Don Pedro will bring trouble to Leonato's house

LEONATO
Never came trouble to my house in the likeness of your Grace. For trouble being gone, comfort should remain; but when you depart from me sorrow abides, and happiness takes his leave.   85

DON PEDRO
You embrace your charge too willingly. (*Indicating* HERO) I think this is your daughter.

Theme: love and marriage

The faithfulness of women is questioned here; this is male joking, but at the expense of women

LEONATO
Her mother hath many times told me so.

BENEDICK
Were you in doubt, sir, that you asked her?

Character

Benedick has a reputation with the ladies

LEONATO
Signior Benedick, no; for then were you a child.   90

DON PEDRO
You have it full, Benedick: we may guess by this what you are being a man. Truly, the lady fathers herself. (*To* HERO) Be happy, lady; for you are like an honourable father.

BENEDICK
If Signior Leonato be her father, she would not have   95
his head on her shoulders for all Messina, as like him
as she is.

DON PEDRO and LEONATO move aside to talk.

BEATRICE
I wonder that you will still be talking, Signior Benedick.
Nobody marks you.

BENEDICK
What, my dear Lady Disdain! Are you yet living?   100

BEATRICE
Is it possible disdain should die while she hath such
meet food to feed it as Signior Benedick? Courtesy itself
must convert to disdain, if you come in her presence.

BENEDICK
Then is courtesy a turncoat. But it is certain I am loved
of all ladies, only you excepted; and I would I could   105
find in my heart that I had not a hard heart, for, truly, I
love none.

BEATRICE
A dear happiness to women: they would else have been
troubled with a pernicious suitor! I thank God and my
cold blood, I am of your humour for that. I had rather   110
hear my dog bark at a crow than a man swear he loves
me.

BENEDICK
God keep your ladyship still in that mind! So some
gentleman or other shall 'scape a predestinate scratched
face.   115

BEATRICE
Scratching could not make it worse, and 'twere such a
face as yours were.

BENEDICK
Well, you are a rare parrot-teacher.

BEATRICE
A bird of my tongue is better than a beast of yours.

Theme: insults
Beatrice begins the battle by telling Benedick he is so boring and unimportant, everyone has stopped listening to him

Character
Benedick admits that he is very popular with women, but is not attached to anyone – a position he enjoys and aims to keep

Language
The harsh sound of a dog barking is more pleasant than words of love; the animal imagery continues in this scene

Language
Benedick does not answer using her name, but insults her by giving her the title of 'Lady Disdain', which suggests she looks down on others

Performance
Benedick should turn his back to Beatrice when she first speaks to him to show that he is not pleased or interested in talking to her

Theme: insults
Beatrice is suggesting Benedick is so ugly a few scratches on his face would not make any difference

Language

Benedick is suggesting that Beatrice's talk is just useless prattle; comparing her to a horse is another insult

BENEDICK

I would my horse had the speed of your tongue, and so 120
good a continuer. But keep your way, a' God's name. I
have done.

BEATRICE

You always end with a jade's trick: I know you of old.

Performance

Benedick should start to walk away, flapping his hands as if he was swotting away a fly; this would show he finds Beatrice irritating and not worth talking to – his comment 'I have done' is dismissing her

Extract 2: Act 2, Scene 1, line 183 to end

Enter DON PEDRO, *with* LEONATO *and* HERO
following

DON PEDRO (*To* BENDICK)
Now signor, where's the Count? Did you
see him?

Performance

Benedick should make his face look very sad to show how Claudio is depressed and melancholic

BENEDICK
Troth, my lord, I have played the part of Lady Fame.   185
I found him here as melancholy as a lodge in a warren.
I told him, and I think I told him true, that your Grace
had got the good will of this young lady; and I offered
him my company to a willow-tree, either to make him
a garland, as being forsaken, or to bind him up a rod, as   190
being worthy to be whipped.

DON PEDRO
To be whipped! What's his fault?

Theme: appearance and reality

Don Pedro has given the impression he is wooing Hero for himself when the reality is he is doing it for Claudio

BENEDICK
The flat transgression of a schoolboy – who being
overjoyed with finding a bird's nest, shows it his
companion, and he steals it.   195

Character

The word 'schoolboy' shows how young and naïve Claudio is

DON PEDRO
Wilt thou make a trust a transgression? The transgression
is in the stealer.

Performance

Benedick should pretend he has a stick in his hand and strike Don Pedro to show that Claudio is angry with him

BENEDICK
Yet it had not been amiss the rod had been made, and
The garland too; for the garland he might have worn
himself, and the rod he might have bestowed on you,   200
who, as I take it, have stolen his bird's nest.

DON PEDRO
I will but teach them to sing, and restore them to the
owner.

Character

Don Pedro has the power and authority to make Claudio and Hero happy

Language

The word 'owner' emphasises that Hero is a possession to be given away

BENEDICK
If their singing answer your saying, but my faith you say
honestly.   205

DON PEDRO
The Lady Beatrice hath a quarrel to you: the gentleman
that danced with her told her she is much wronged by
you.

Theme: battle of the sexes

Beatrice continues to wage war on Benedick

Language

The repetition of 'I' emphasises how Beatrice has hurt Benedick's feelings

Language

The reference to Beatrice's words being daggers shows how effective she has been in wounding Benedick's male pride

Character

Don Pedro does the same thing and calls Beatrice 'she', which shows he sympathises with Benedick

Performance

Benedick should fall to his knees and clasp his hands together to plead to escape from Beatrice; this shows how desperate he has become to get away from her

BENEDICK

O, she misused me past the endurance of a block! An oak but with one green leaf on it would have answered 210 her. My very visor began to assume life and scold with her. She told me, not thinking I had been myself, that I was the Prince's jester, that I was duller than a great thaw – huddling jest upon jest with such impossible conveyance upon me that I stood like a man at a mark, 215 with a whole army shooting at me. She speaks poniards, and every word stabs. If her breath were as terrible as her terminations, there were no living near he: she would infect to the north star. I would not marry her, though she were endowed with all that Adam had left 220 him before he transgressed. She would have made Hercules have turned spit, yea, and have cleft his club to make the fire too. Come, talk not of her. You shall find her the infernal Até in good apparel. I would to God some scholar would conjure her. For certainly, while 225 she is here, a man may live as quiet in hell as in a sanctuary, and people sin upon purpose because they would go thither. So indeed, all disquiet, horror, and perturbation follows her.

Enter CLAUDIO *and* BEATRICE.

DON PEDRO
Look, here she comes.   230

BENEDICK
Will your Grace command me any service to the world's end? I will go on the slightest errand now to the Antipodes that you can devise to send me on. I will fetch you a tooth-picker now from the furthest inch of Asia; bring you the length of Prester John's foot; fetch 235 you a hair off the great Cham's beard; do you any embassage to the Pigmies – rather than hold three word's conference with this harpy. You have no employment for me?

DON PEDRO
None, but to desire your good company.   240

BENEDICK
O God, sir, here's a dish I love not. I cannot endure my Lady Tongue.
Exit BENEDICK

DON PEDRO
Come, lady, come. You have lost the heart of Signior Benedick.

Language

Benedick cannot use Beatrice's name. He refers to her as 'she' or 'her', which shows how angry he is with her.

Performance

Benedick should quickly walk back and forth in front of Don Pedro to show how angry he is; every time he says 'I' he should point his finger at himself to show he is the one who has been most hurt

Character

Don Pedro shows he is fond of Benedick and enjoys his company

Theme: love

Don Pedro is suggesting that Beatrice is at fault because she has made Benedick lose his affection for her by her sharp comments to him

BEATRICE
Indeed, my lord, he lent it me awhile, and I gave him   245
use for it, a double heart for his single one. Marry, once
before he won it of me with a <u>false dice</u>: therefore your
Grace may well say I have lost it.

DON PEDRO
<u>You have put him down</u>, lady, <u>you have put him down</u>.

BEATRICE
So I would not he should do me, my lord, lest I should   250
prove the <u>mother of fools</u>. I have brought Count
Claudio, whom you sent me to seek.

DON PEDRO
Why, how now, Count! Wherefore are you sad?

CLAUDIO
Not sad, my lord.

DON PEDRO
How then? Sick?   255

CLAUDIO
Neither, my lord.

BEATRICE
The Count is neither sad, nor sick, nor merry, nor well;
but civil count, civil as an <u>orange</u>, and <u>something of that</u>
<u>jealous complexion</u>.

DON PEDRO
I' faith, lady, I think your blazon to be true; though, I'll   260
be sworn, if he be so, his conceit is false. Here, Claudio,
I have wooed in thy name, and fair Hero is won. I have
broke with her father, and his good will obtained. Name
the day of marriage, and God give thee joy!

LEONATO
<u>Count, take of me my daughter, and with her my</u>   265
<u>fortunes</u>. His Grace hath made the match and all grace
say Amen to it!

BEATRICE
Speak, Count, 'tis your cue.

CLAUDIO
Silence is the perfectest herald of <u>joy</u>. I were but little
<u>happy</u>, if I could say how much. Lady, as you are mine,   270
I am yours: I give away myself for you and <u>dote</u> upon
the exchange.

BEATRICE
Speak, cousin – or, if you cannot, stop his mouth with a kiss, and let not him speak neither.

DON PEDRO
In faith, lady, you have a merry heart.   275

BEATRICE
Yea, my lord; I thank it, poor fool, it keeps on the windy side of care. <u>My cousin tells him in his ear that he is in her heart.</u>

CLAUDIO
And so she doth, cousin.

BEATRICE
<u>Good Lord, for alliance! Thus goes everyone to the</u>   280
<u>world but I, and I am sunburnt. I may sit in a corner and</u>
<u>cry 'Heigh-ho for a husband!'</u>

DON PEDRO
Lady Beatrice, <u>I will get you one.</u>

BEATRICE
<u>I would rather have one of your father's getting. Hath</u>
<u>Your Grace ne'er a brother like you? Your father got</u>   285
<u>excellent husbands, if a maid could come by them.</u>

DON PEDRO
Will you have *me*, lady?

BEATRICE
<u>No, my lord, unless I might have another for working</u>
<u>days. Your Grace is too costly to wear every day. But I</u>
<u>beseech your Grace, pardon me: I was born to speak all</u>   290
<u>mirth and no matter.</u>

DON PEDRO
Your silence most offends me, and to be merry best becomes you; for, out of question, you were born in a merry hour.

BEATRICE
<u>No, sure, my lord, my mother cried.</u> But then there was 295 a star danced, and under that was I born. Cousins, God give you joy!

LEONATO
Niece, will you look to those things I told you of?

Performance
Hero and Claudio should move away from the others, hold each other, kiss, gaze into one another's eyes and whisper to show they are only interested in each other

Character
Beatrice lets her true feelings show when she wishes she had a husband; she wants to be loved in the same way as other women

Character
Beatrice tries to make a joke out of her request for a husband, which suggests she is embarrassed by her revelation

Performance
This line should be said quietly and in a sad tone to show that Beatrice understands how her mother suffered during childbirth; the second line should be lively to show Beatrice is joking again

Theme: marriage
Don Pedro thinks it is an easy job to find a husband for Beatrice; there is no mention of love

Language
Beatrice makes light of Don Pedro's proposal by likening him to an expensive dress that should not be worn every day (she would need an ordinary one for that); her wit gets her out of a delicate situation

BEATRICE
I cry you mercy, uncle. (*To* DON PEDRO) By your Grace's
pardon.   300

Exit BEATRICE.

DON PEDRO
By my troth, <u>a pleasant-spirited lady</u>.

LEONATO
There's little of the melancholy element in her, my lord.
She is never sad but when she sleeps, and not ever sad
then: for I have heard my daughter say, she hath often
dreamt of unhappiness and waked herself with laughing.   305

DON PEDRO
She cannot endure to hear tell of a husband.

LEONATO
O, by no means. She mocks all her wooers out of suit.

DON PEDRO
She were an <u>excellent wife for Benedick</u>.

LEONATO
<u>O Lord, my lord, if they were but a week married, they</u>
<u>would talk themselves mad.</u>   310

DON PEDRO
Count Claudio, when mean you to go to church?

CLAUDIO
Tomorrow, my lord. <u>Time goes on crutches, till love have</u>
<u>all his rites.</u>

LEONATO
<u>Not till Monday, my dear son, which is hence a just</u>
<u>seven-night – and a time too brief, too, to have all things</u>315
<u>answer my mind.</u>

DON PEDRO
Come, you shake the head at so long a breathing – but
<u>I</u> warrant thee, Claudio, the time shall not go dully by
us. <u>I</u> will in the interim undertake one of Hercules'
labours – which is, to bring Signior Benedick and the   320
Lady Beatrice into a mountain of affection, the one with
the other. <u>I</u> would fain have it a match; and <u>I</u> doubt not
but to fashion it, if you three will but minister such
assistance as <u>I</u> shall give you direction.

Character

Don Pedro's comment is in sharp contrast to what Benedick said about Beatrice earlier in the scene; Don Pedro can see Beatrice's good qualities

Theme: marriage

Don Pedro can see that Benedick needs an intelligent, sharp-witted woman to be his wife

Theme: marriage

Leonato thinks that marriage between Beatrice and Benedick would be a mistake

Language

Claudio shows his impatience to get married by using the image of time as being a cripple and taking too long to get to the right place

Performance

Leonato should shake his head to emphasise that he will not agree to an early wedding

Language

The use of 'I' by Don Pedro shows how powerful he is; he has decided he wants Beatrice and Benedick to marry, and is determined it will happen according to his plan

Character

Hero's willingness to help her cousin shows she is a kind and thoughtful person

Performance

Don Pedro should place his hands on Hero's shoulders to show he is in charge and she must do as he says

Character

Don Pedro shows he has an arrogant side to his character by claiming he is better at making people fall in love than Cupid is.

LEONATO
My lord, I am for you, though it cost me ten nights'   325
watchings.

CLAUDIO
And I, my lord.

DON PEDRO
And you too, gentle Hero?

HERO
I will do my modest office, my lord, to help my cousin
to a good husband.   330

DON PEDRO
And Benedick is not the unhopefullest husband that I
know. Thus far can I praise him: he is of a noble strain,
of approved valour and confirmed honesty. I will teach
you how to humour your cousin, that she shall fall in
love with Benedick. And I, with your two helps, will so 335
practise on Benedick that, in despite of his quick wit
and his queasy stomach, he shall fall in love with
Beatrice. If we can do this, Cupid is no longer an
archer: his glory shall be ours, for we are the only love
gods. Go in with me, and I will tell you my drift.   340
Exeunt.

Character

Don Pedro lists the masculine qualities he sees in Benedick that will make him a good husband

Character Grid

Working with a partner, think and talk about the statements in the first column. Then fill in your responses in the appropriate column, giving evidence from the set extracts. Explain and explore your thinking. The first line has been completed for you as an example. Compare your completed sheets with the sheets of other pupils.

Beatrice and Benedick

Statement	Response	Yes/No	Evidence	Explanation	Exploration
Beatrice defeats Benedick in the 'skirmish of wit'.	Definitely. Yes, on balance. Not really. No way.	Yes	'Is it possible disdain should die while she hath such meet food to feed it as Signior Benedick?' (Beatrice, Act 1, Scene 1, lines 101–102) 'I cannot endure my Lady Tongue.' (Benedick, Act 2, Scene 1, lines 241–2) 'You have put him down, lady ...' (Don Pedro, Act 2, Scene 1, line 249)	Beatrice is quick-witted enough to beat Benedick in the 'merry war' (Act 1, Scene 1, line 51) in the eyes of others.	Beatrice says more, chooses more powerful images and speaks with more aggression than Benedick.
It is clear from these extracts that Beatrice and Benedick will end up together.	Definitely. Yes, on balance. Not really. No way.				
Beatrice's mood is just the same in both extracts.	Definitely. Yes, on balance. Not really. No way.				
It is clear from these extracts that Benedick is seen by other men as a good friend.	Definitely. Yes, on balance. Not really. No way.				
Don Pedro thinks that Beatrice and Benedick deserve each other.	Definitely. Yes, on balance. Not really. No way.				
We accept Benedick's view of Beatrice as 'Lady Tongue'.	Definitely. Yes, on balance. Not really. No way.				
The audience is more interested in Benedick and Beatrice than in Claudio and Hero.	Definitely. Yes, on balance. Not really. No way.				

Focus on character

Highlight the key words in the tables below and fill in the blank rows with your own points, quotations and personal responses.

Extract 1: Act 1, Scene 1, lines 1 to 123

Points	Quotations	Personal responses
Beatrice is rude about absent Benedick. Leonato and the others are used to, and amused by, the 'merry war' between Beatrice and Benedick.	Beatrice: '… is Signior Mountanto returned from the wars?' (line 25); '… how many hath he killed and eaten in these wars? (lines 35–6).	We wonder why insulting Benedick matters so much to her. We expect the 'skirmish of wit' between them to be at the comic heart of the play.
Beatrice mounts an immediate verbal assault on Benedick; her first words to him are a vicious put-down to which he responds defensively.	Beatrice: 'I wonder that you will still be talking, Signior Benedick. Nobody marks you' (lines 98–9). Benedick: 'What, my dear Lady Disdain!' (line 100); '… it is certain I am loved of all ladies, only you excepted' (lines 104–105).	Benedick protests so much his prowess as a lover that we detect a hint of self-doubt behind Benedick's bravado.
Beatrice rejects all men, not just Benedick, and puts them below animals. Benedick chooses to end the fighting talk by retreating. Beatrice suggests she has known Benedick for some time.	Benedick: 'I would my horse had the speed of your tongue' (line 120). Beatrice: 'You always end with a jade's trick: I know you of old' (line 123).	This signals the 'beastliness' in all men to the audience. Beatrice wins their first verbal joust. We wonder what their relationship once was and will become.

Extract 2: Act 2, Scene 1, line 183 to end

Points	Quotations	Personal responses
Benedick has been hurt by Beatrice's words and describes her with comic exaggeration. Don Pedro feels sorry for his word-wounded friend. Beatrice refers to when she felt differently.	Benedick: 'She speaks poniards, and every word stabs' (lines 216–7); 'I cannot endure my Lady Tongue' (lines 241–2); 'I would not marry her' (line 219); Don Pedro: 'You have lost the heart of Signior Benedick' (lines 243–4); Beatrice: 'Marry, once before he won it of me with false dice' (lines 246–7).	Benedick has been hurt by Beatrice's insults, but we are amused. We wonder what happened before and if it will happen again.
Claudio is full of love rather than full just of language. Beatrice comments ruefully on being single, but declines the Duke's not-very-serious marriage offer.	Claudio: 'Silence is the perfectest herald of joy. I were but little happy, if I could say how much' (lines 269–70). Beatrice: 'I may sit in the corner and cry "Heigh-ho for a husband!"' (lines 281–2) Don Pedro: 'Lady Beatrice, I will get you one' (line 283). Beatrice: 'Your Grace is too costly to wear every day' (line 289).	Claudio's simple tone contrasts with the world of wit. Beatrice fears she has overstepped the mark in refusing the Duke's joking offer.
Don Pedro and others have a positive view of Benedick.	Don Pedro: '… Benedick is not the unhopefullest husband that I know. … he is of noble strain, of approved valour and confirmed honesty' (lines 331–3).	We later see the justice of this estimate of Benedick's virtues.

Focus on theme

Decide which theme is illustrated by each quotation and jot it down. Fill in the blank rows with your own points, quotations and personal responses.

Extract 1: Act 1, Scene 1, lines 1 to 123

Points	Quotations	Personal responses
Beatrice insults Benedick by saying he is more interested in his stomach than in fighting.	Beatrice: 'I pray you, how many hath he killed and eaten in these wars?' (lines 35–6).	She attacks and belittles him, poking fun at the male world of war, honour and chivalry.
Beatrice suggests Benedick is more like a disease than a true friend to other soldiers.	Beatrice: 'O Lord, he will hang upon him like a disease' (line 69).	We see how bitter her attacks are. Their friendship is more an appearance than reality.
Benedick behaves arrogantly and has lots of boastful remarks.	Benedick: 'But it is certain I am loved of all ladies, only you excepted' (lines 104–105).	The male ego is exposed so we can see what Beatrice dislikes about him.
Beatrice says she doesn't ever want to get married.	Beatrice: 'I had rather hear my dog bark at a crow than a man swear he loves me' (lines 110–11).	Through this extreme comment it is clear they won't love easily. This is in strong contrast with Claudio and Hero.

Extract 2: Act 2, Scene 1, line 183 to end

Points	Quotations	Personal responses
The insults between Beatrice and Benedick become more cruel in Extract 2.	Benedick: '… she would infect the north star' (lines 218–19); 'So, indeed, all disquiet, horror, and perturbation follows her' (lines 228–9).	They appear to hate each other but we suspect that will change.
Beatrice is suddenly serious when she says how Benedick tricked her.	Beatrice: 'Marry, once before he won it of me with false dice' (lines 246–7).	The truth about her past emerges and we see her real feelings.
Leonato offers to Claudio his daughter in marriage.	Leonato: 'Count, take of me my daughter, and with her my fortunes' (lines 265–6).	The place of women is clearly shown. Hero is like a possession to be traded between the men.
The plot to make Beatrice and Benedick love each other is planned, though the men know it will be hard to achieve.	Don Pedro: 'I will in the interim undertake one of Hercules' labours' (lines 319–20); '… he shall fall in love with (lines 337–8); '… we are the only love-gods' (lines 339–40).	The men don't think of Beatrice, only of Benedick and their own glory.

Focus on language

Highlight the key words in the tables below and fill in the blank rows with your own points, quotations and personal responses.

Extract 1: Act 1, Scene 1, lines 1 to 123

Points	Quotations	Personal responses
The repetition of words like 'joy' show that the opening scene has a happy atmosphere.	Leonato: 'How much better it is to weep at joy than to joy at weeping! (lines 23–4).	The atmosphere at the start of the play relaxes the audience.
The scene is written in prose.	Leonato: 'Never came trouble to my house in the likeness of your Grace. For trouble being gone, comfort should remain; but when you depart from me sorrow abides, and happiness takes his leave' (lines 82–5).	We see here an honest, relaxed and polite society.
When Beatrice is talking about Benedick she does not use his name and refers to him as 'he'.	Beatrice: 'Who is his companion now? He hath every month a new sworn brother' (lines 59–60).	Beatrice's use of pronouns is another way of insulting him to make him seem unimportant.
Leonato uses words of war to describe Beatrice and Benedick's relationship.	Leonato: 'There is a kind of merry war betwixt Signior Benedick and her. They never meet but there's a skirmish of wit between them' (lines 50–52).	In contrast to real wars, Benedick and Beatrice enjoy their clashes.

Extract 2: Act 2, Scene 1, line 183 to end

Points	Quotations	Personal responses
Benedick and Don Pedro use language about Hero that makes her sound like a possession.	Benedick: '… have stolen his bird's nest' (line 201) Don Pedro: 'I will … restore them to the owner' (202–203).	Men think they have the power to treat women as possessions.
Benedick has been hurt by his encounter with Beatrice in the masked ball.	Benedick: 'She speaks poniards, and every word stabs' (lines 216–7).	Beatrice's wit is as sharp as a dagger and never fails to wound Benedick's ego.
Beatrice has been wronged in love by Benedick.	Beatrice: 'Indeed, my lord, he lent it me awhile, and I gave him use for it, a double heart for his single one' (lines 245–6).	Benedick had no intention of staying faithful to Beatrice. She chides herself for being naive.
Leonato is delighted his daughter is to marry Claudio and follows the protocols for announcing the engagement.	Leonato: 'Count, take of me my daughter, and with her my fortunes. His Grace has made the match and all say Amen to it!' (lines 265–7).	This formal announcement emphasises the legal and religious significance of marriage.

Focus on performance

Highlight the key words in the tables below and then fill in the blank rows with your own points, quotations and personal responses.

Extract 1: Act 1, Scene 1, lines 1 to 123

Points	Quotations	Personal responses
Beatrice is a woman not afraid of tackling men on their own terms.	Messenger: 'I will hold friends with you, lady' (line 74).	Beatrice mimics the tone of the Messenger and enjoys confusing him with her wit, but then takes pity on him, so we don't see her as cruel – just clever.
Beatrice should ask about Benedick in a jokingly insulting fashion to conceal her interest in him.	Beatrice: ' … is Signior Mountanto returned from the wars …?' (lines 25–6); 'He hath every month a new sworn brother' (lines 59–60).	We realise the play is about two enemies falling in love.
Benedick should respond sarcastically when Beatrice insults him, then start boasting of his conquests.	Beatrice: 'Nobody marks you.' Benedick: 'What, my dear Lady Disdain! Are you yet living?' (lines 99–100); 'But it is certain I am loved of all ladies, only you excepted …' (lines 104–105).	Benedick resorts to giving Beatrice a nasty title, and disguises his uncertainty by boasting.
The two catch fire verbally, with one's insults sparking off the other's response.	Benedick: 'Well, you are a rare parrot-teacher.' Beatrice: 'A bird of my tongue is better than a beast of yours' (lines 118–19).	Both should seem to enjoy this repartee, but Benedick is the first to seek escape and we see Beatrice as the verbal victor.

Extract 2: Act 2, Scene 1, line 183 to end

Points	Quotations	Personal responses
Beatrice should look shocked when she hears Benedick call her 'Lady Tongue'. Her tone should be angry and hurt.	Beatrice: '… he won it of me with false dice' (line 247).	The word 'false' should be said strongly to emphasise why she is bitter about Benedick's attitude to women.
Beatrice should be happy for Hero, because she has given her heart to Claudio, but suddenly changes her tone.	Beatrice: 'Good Lord, for alliance!' (line 280).	This sudden exclamation shows she knows that marriage is based on fortune, not love.
When Don Pedro offers to marry Beatrice, she should daringly move close to him and flirt.	Beatrice: 'Your Grace is too costly to wear every day' (line 199).	She should pause and look at him, then curtsy when she realises she has gone too far (' … pardon me').
In Extract 1 Beatrice has a merry tone, but she is serious in her attitude to men.	Beatrice: ' …my mother cried … a star danced' (lines 295–6).	She should speak sadly and dramatically, then suddenly change the mood with 'but' and twirl round like a star.

The Key Stage 3 Shakespeare test

How to approach the test

Remember that:

- The Shakespeare test accounts for 18 out of the 50 marks for reading. You gain marks by showing you understand and have responded to Shakespeare.
- The way you write matters because it enables you to make your points effectively, but you will not be judged on how well you write. No marks are given (or taken off) for spelling or expression.
- The extracts you will have to write about will be printed in the test paper. Don't make the mistake of writing about all the set scenes – concentrate on those two extracts.
- PQR (**P**oint, **Q**uotation, **R**esponse) is better than PEE (**P**oint, **E**xplanation, **E**xample) because it includes your personal reaction to the play.
- Short quotations are better than long ones because they save you time in the test.

And, by the way …
since you will have to write about both extracts, you are not likely to be asked to focus on characters like the Messenger who doesn't appear at all in Extract 2 or Hero who appears only briefly.

Revision

You can use this book to help with your preparation for the test by:

- looking back at the illustrated outline of the play on pages 4 and 5 to remind yourself of the sequence of events

- making sure that you are familiar with the quotations by and about Beatrice and Benedick, and that you are used to telling other people your thoughts about them

- getting your head round the four 'big ideas' of character, language, themes and performance by talking with others about the points and quotations on pages 19–22

- planning answers to some or all of the sample questions on page 26

- working out the strengths (and there are many) of the sample answer, and what could be done to improve it

- looking at the marking criteria on page 25 enough to understand why marks are awarded by the examiners, and making sure that you can do what is needed.

Top 10 tips for the test

1. Make sure you are familiar with the layout and style of questions by looking at tests from previous years.

2. Read the question aloud in your head two or three times until you realise what it is really asking you to do.

3. Keep in mind performances of the play that you have seen in the theatre or on video, and remember what it was like acting out the set scenes with other people.

4. It is better to explore a few points in depth and discuss the effect of language in detail than to offer a series of general comments.

5. Don't ever just tell the story – answer the question.

6. Time spent on planning is time well spent. Practise doing a plan in five minutes so that in the real test you can create a plan within ten minutes.

7. Plan so that your main points are in a sensible order that responds to the question.

8. Provide evidence in quotations or refer to what happens and what is said to support your points. *(Remember not to waste time copying out long quotations but do make sure you comment on the effect of the language.)*

9. Make sure that your conclusion relates back to the question.

10. Leave time (but not too much!) at the end of the test to read through what you have written.

What do I need to remember about how the Shakespeare paper will be marked?

Your understanding of *Much Ado About Nothing* is assessed only for reading.

- No marks are given (or taken off) for spelling or expression, but the way you write does matter because it enables you to make your points effectively.

- You are not expected to write about the play as a whole, but to refer to the extracts given on the test paper. These extracts will be taken from the set scenes which are on pages 6 to 17 of this book.

What will the question be on?

The question on *Much Ado About Nothing* should be on **one** of the areas (or 'big ideas') below, although you can refer to the other areas as part of your answer:

- why characters behave as they do in the extracts given

- the impact of the language used in the extracts

- ideas, themes and issues that are relevant to the extracts

- how these extracts might be performed in the theatre.

Key Stage 3 marking

How will my answer be marked?

Answers on Shakespeare are not directly related to levels. Instead they are allocated to mark bands, and a decision about which marks determine the final level is taken during the marking process.

There is no substitute for looking at the details of the Key Stage 3 mark scheme issued by QCA, but the characteristics of different mark bands for a question on character are set out below.

Band	General Characteristics	What will that look like?
1	A few simple facts and opinions about the focus of the question. Some parts of the extracts may be re-told or copied and answers may be only partly relevant.	Comments remain on a general level and may reveal only partial understanding of task and text. The treatment of extracts is likely to be uneven, with much paraphrase and unselective use of quotation.
2	Some awareness of the more obvious aspects of the question. Some broad references to the way character(s) speak or behave.	Some evidence of implicit awareness of more obvious aspects of a character's behaviour, with some attempt at exemplification or explanation. The treatment of the two extracts may be unbalanced and simple references may not be linked with comments. Little, if any, comment on the effect of characters' use of language, although there may be reference to some words or phrases.
3	Shows general understanding of characters' feeling and of the way language reveals character and refers to textual evidence.	Secure general understanding of the impression an audience might have of characters and how they develop. Points are generally illustrated by relevant references to the text but comments are likely to be repeated rather than developed. There may be reliance on paraphrase rather than analysis. Limited comment (if any) on the effects of language.
4	Shows awareness of characters' feelings and how this is shown through language and its effects.	May provide some discussion of the impressions an audience might get of a character from the way they speak or behave. Relevant references from both extracts will be included and there should be a secure understanding of the broader context of the play. Explicit, if limited, comment on the effects of a character's use of language would be expected.
5	Clear focus on the question asked, with understanding of the way language is used and of its effects. Well chosen references to the text justify comments as part of an overall argument.	A relevant and focused answer which engages confidently with both extracts. Aspects of the text will be explored, not just explained, in ways that show a wider understanding of the play's development. The selection of well-chosen references builds into a sustained argument which includes comment on the dramatic effect of the language used.
6	Coherent analysis of characters' actions and attitudes. Appreciation of the features and effects of language. Comments and precisely selected references to the text are integrated into well-developed argument.	A focused and developed analysis of the impression created by a character through language and action on stage. The answer engages analytically with both extracts, showing insight into the less obvious aspects of the text and an ability to contextualise ideas. Appreciation of the features and effects of language is well supported by integrated references. There may be recognition of the possibility of different interpretations of the text.

Sample questions

Themes
- Appearance and reality
- Honour and insult
- Male and female
- Love and marriage

- What do these two extracts show about attitudes to love and marriage?
- What do these two extracts suggest about the differences between appearance and reality?
- What differences might the audience notice between the insults and how characters react to them in the first and second extracts?
- What do these two extracts tell you about the relationships between men and women?

Language
- In these two extracts, how does Beatrice use language to win 'the merry war' with men?
- What differences do you notice between Beatrice's use of language in these two extracts?

Character
- In these two extracts how does Beatrice show that she is not afraid to compete in the world of men?
- In these two extracts is an audience likely to sympathise more with Beatrice or with Benedick?
- How does Benedick show that honour is important to him in these extracts?
- How does Beatrice reveal her feelings about men in these two extracts?

Performance
- What advice would you give to the actor playing Benedick on how to respond to Beatrice in these two extracts?
- If you were directing this play, what advice would you give to the actor playing Beatrice on how to respond to the men?

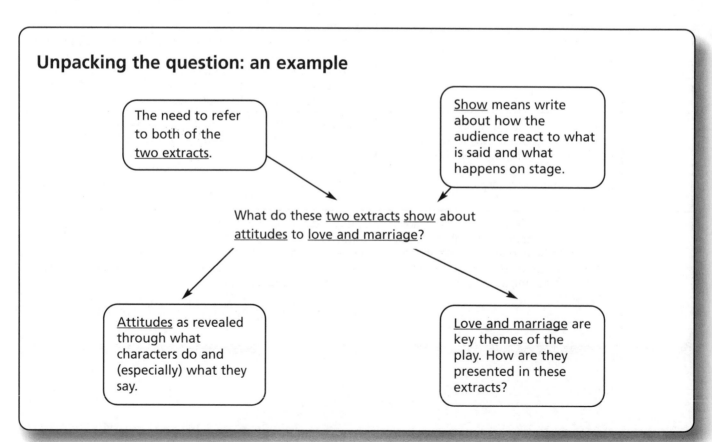

Unpacking the question: an example

The need to refer to both of the <u>two extracts</u>.

<u>Show</u> means write about how the audience react to what is said and what happens on stage.

What do these <u>two extracts</u> <u>show</u> about <u>attitudes</u> to <u>love and marriage</u>?

<u>Attitudes</u> as revealed through what characters do and (especially) what they say.

<u>Love and marriage</u> are key themes of the play. How are they presented in these extracts?

Sample answer with examiner's comments

If you were directing this play, what advice would you give to the actor playing Beatrice on how to respond to the men?

Understanding of how Beatrice should speak

Why?

Generalised advice

Precise quotation with fuller explanation needed

Selected quotation and some awareness of why the actor should speak and act in this way

My advice to an actress playing Beatrice is that she should speak <u>sarcastically</u> to Benedick when she says 'no one marks you' because she is angry with him. He has been joking with Don Pedro about Hero's mother. She should try to explain that he has no 'courtesy' but he changes the subject and boasts that he does not love any woman.

Because he is so conceited Beatrice should face up to him in the centre of the stage and call him 'pernicious' in a loud voice. In extract two Beatrice tells the audience why she is so bitter about Benedick because he has loved her and left her, so she should proudly tell him that she never wants a man to love her.

They are both ready for an argument and pick up each others words and as Beatrice throws the words back at Benedick she should speak faster and faster and her tone should become vicious as she spits out 'parrot' and 'beast'. She should laugh and mock Benedick when he has the last word and goes out.

Beatrice has spoken to Benedick when they were both masked. In extract 2 he is shocked and angry because she had called him a fool and he is insulting her in front of the lords. He says she is worse than hell and Beatrice comes in and hears him call her a 'harpy'. I think even Beatrice is embarrassed when everyone is laughing because he says he would go to the ends of the earth to escape her.

She should look furious and use a bitter tone when she says that Benedick played for her heart using 'false dice'. The audience can see why Beatrice has such a war of words with men because she is like a poor Cinderella who will never get a husband.

She should flirt with Don Pedro when he offers to marry her and show that she is full of fun which he likes. She should stroke his jacket and say he is 'too costly' in a daring tone. I think she knows that she has gone too far and she should curtsey and ask pardon in a mock polite way. When Leonato tells her to go she should dance out.

Broad advice about how Beatrice speaks. Selected quotation, but needs fuller explanation

Fuller explanation needed

Relevant points made

Band 3/4

This essay refers to both extracts and shows understanding of the ways an actor playing Beatrice should show different ways of reacting to her relationship with Benedick. There is some general comment and broad advice illustrated by relevant quotation. (Band 3) At the end there is an awareness of why Beatrice speaks as she does with clear advice supported by relevant quotation (Band 4).

Planning your answer

Spend at least five minutes on planning in the test. The time available for planning in the test is limited, so it needs to be used well. The question is likely to be on one of the following:

- why characters behave as they do in the extracts given
- the impact of the language used in the extracts
- ideas, themes and issues that are relevant to the extracts
- how these extracts might be performed in the theatre.

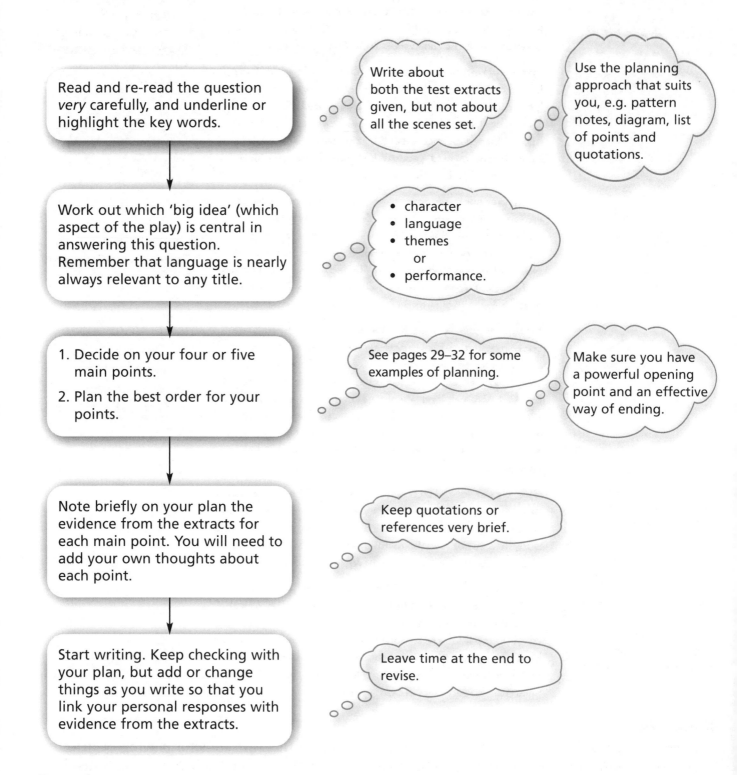

Read and re-read the question *very* carefully, and underline or highlight the key words.

Write about both the test extracts given, but not about all the scenes set.

Use the planning approach that suits you, e.g. pattern notes, diagram, list of points and quotations.

Work out which 'big idea' (which aspect of the play) is central in answering this question. Remember that language is nearly always relevant to any title.

- character
- language
- themes
  or
- performance.

1. Decide on your four or five main points.
2. Plan the best order for your points.

See pages 29–32 for some examples of planning.

Make sure you have a powerful opening point and an effective way of ending.

Note briefly on your plan the evidence from the extracts for each main point. You will need to add your own thoughts about each point.

Keep quotations or references very brief.

Start writing. Keep checking with your plan, but add or change things as you write so that you link your personal responses with evidence from the extracts.

Leave time at the end to revise.

Remember
Marking 300 similar answers does get boring, so examiners appreciate a personal voice in an answer that does not just state the obvious.

Planning a character answer

Number the four main points (in bold) in the order that you would put them in an answer.

We enjoy Beatrice's humour 'How many hath he killed and eaten in these wars?' and her wit, which bewilders the Messenger and defeats Benedick. However, we might agree with Leonato that 'you tax Signior Benedick too much' since her put-down ('Nobody marks you') is pretty vicious. When she says 'I know you of old' we are intrigued.

We admire Benedick's loyalty to Claudio since he risks upsetting the Duke on behalf of his friend. Benedick has been so hurt by Beatrice's 'poniards' that he avoids 'my Lady Tongue'.

We hear of Benedick before we see him, but we are left wondering since the harsh views of Beatrice contradict the messenger's praise.

We are told that Benedick 'wears his faith but as the fashion of his hat', so the last thing we expect from him is loyalty.

Explain how words and actions from Extract 2 could influence an audience's attitude to these two characters. Illustrate by picking out words or phrases from the text.

Explain why certain words and actions in Extract 1 have the effect on the audience that they do. Illustrate by picking out words or phrases from the text.

Others see Beatrice as a 'pleasant spirited lady' and enjoy her 'merry war' with Benedick.

In these two extracts is an audience likely to sympathise more with Beatrice or with Benedick?

Beatrice implies that she and Benedick were once close. She appears to share the joy of the lovers, and says 'Thus goes everyone to the world but I'.

We see Beatrice as a wickedly witty lady, not overshadowed by men or status, whose own words reveal her fascination with Benedick, 'Signior Mountanto'.

How does an audience learn about these characters? (Comment with understanding on character and behaviour because of what is seen or what is said by them or about them.)

Give your personal response to both sections. Identify and comment on how you think an audience might respond differently to the two characters.

Initial impressions of Benedick:
'He hath every month a new sworn brother' (Beatrice).
'He hath done good service, lady, in these wars' (Messenger).

We admire Beatrice for her wit and wonder whether her verbal attacks on Benedick conceal or reveal her feelings for him.

Benedick is a target for Beatrice's barbed wit, and we do not know how far he deserves what she says of him. The Duke thinks him 'not the unhopefullest husband'

Planning a theme answer

Number the four main points (in bold) in the order that you would put them in an answer.

The relationship between Beatrice and Benedick is quite unlike Hero and Claudio's because Beatrice stands up to Benedick and behaves like his equal. This was unusual in such a male-dominated world. She criticises him and makes fun of him: 'I wonder that you will still be talking, Signior Benedick. Nobody marks you.'

The typical relationship between a father and daughter at that time is shown by the way Leonato treats Hero as his property: 'Count, take of me my daughter.' The men deal with the women between them.

In Extract 2, Benedick can't bear to hear her any more. It is clear that his male ego can't cope with her as his equal in argument: 'I cannot endure my Lady Tongue.'

Behind the wit and fierce comments Beatrice has been hurt by the way Benedick has treated her in the past. She says 'he lent it me awhile' talking of Benedick's love. This shows that even the strongest person can be upset by cruel treatment by the opposite sex.

Explain what the relationship between Claudio and Hero shows about men and women. Illustrate by picking out words or phrases from the text.

Explain what the relationship between Beatrice and Benedick shows about men and women. Illustrate by picking out words or phrases from the text.

What do these two extracts tell you about the relationship between men and women?

The power of love between men and women is shown clearly when Claudio isn't able to speak when he knows he is to marry Hero: 'Silence is the perfectest herald of joy.'

Beatrice doesn't take Benedick's actions in war seriously 'how many hath he killed and eaten in these wars' making fun of the world of men.

Give examples of the different views of men and women in the two extracts.

The audience admire Beatrice for standing up to men and successfully arguing with Benedick: 'I have done.'

Show awareness of the audience response by identifying and commenting on the impact on the audience.

The men use women as a source of sexual humour such as when Leonato makes a joke about whether Hero is really his daughter when she is listening: 'Her mother hath many times told me so.'

The plot to trick Benedick and Beatrice into loving each other shows a male view that love between men and women is something to be made a game of. They don't think about how Beatrice might feel if it goes wrong. 'We are the only love gods' shows how arrogant the men are thinking they can be like Cupid.

The contrast between Hero's meekness and the lively relationship between Beatrice and Benedick allows the audience to compare different relationships.

The strength of Beatrice and Benedick's dislike for each other will make the audience very keen to see if the plot to get them to love each other will actually work and they will fall in love with each other.

Planning a language answer

Number the four main points (in bold) in the order that you would put them in an answer.

Beatrice confuses the messenger with her uncomplimentary name for Benedick – 'Signior Mountanto'. Beatrice cannot bring herself to use Benedick's name, so she uses a name that sounds rude and has sexual overtones.

'Nobody marks you' Beatrice belittles Benedick in their first encounter. This wins Benedick's attention as well as telling him he is boring and unimportant.

The Messenger realises she is more than a match for him: 'I will hold friends with you lady.'

Beatrice jokes about Benedick being like a disease. 'If he have caught the Benedick, it will cost him a thousand pound ere 'a be cured.' She ridicules his name, suggesting that having him as a friend is a curse.

Show how Beatrice 'defeats' Benedick in particular. Illustrate by picking out words or phrases from the text.

Explain how Beatrice speaks to men and about men. Illustrate by picking out words or phrases from the first extract.

Benedick: 'She speaks poniards, and every word stabs.' As the audience realise, Beatrice's wit is as sharp as a dagger and never fails to damage Benedick's male pride and ego.

In these two extracts how does Beatrice use language to win 'the merry war' with men?

Beatrice flirts with Don Pedro and impresses him with her wit: 'Your silence most offends me, and to be merry best becomes you.' He decides she would make an 'excellent wife' for Benedick, his trusted companion.

Give examples of the different ways Beatrice uses language in Extract 2.

Show awareness of the audience response by identifying and commenting on the impact Beatrice's language has on the audience.

Beatrice points out to Don Pedro that Benedick once won her heart but he did not play fairly with her: 'He won it of me with false dice.'

Beatrice teases Claudio about being jealous: 'civil as an orange, and something of that jealous complexion'. She tells Don Pedro Claudio is jealous, and Don Pedro acknowledges that she is right.

When Benedick escapes 'my Lady Tongue' the audience have some sympathy for him, and might agree with Leonato, who sends her out of harm's way because he thinks she has over-stepped the mark with Don Pedro.

Planning a performance answer

Number the four main points (in bold) in the order that you would put them in an answer.

Benedick should sneer as he says she is a 'parrot' with an unstoppable 'tongue' strutting out having had the last word. The squabble becomes nasty as he warns the audience that he could get a 'scratched face'. A verbal tennis match takes place with both characters picking up each other's words and throwing insults back.

Benedick should be obviously shaken by what Beatrice said when she was masked. His long speech should be spoken over-dramatically, using an injured tone as he pictures himself attacked by arrows and stabbed by 'poniards'.

When Beatrice insults him for joking about Hero's mother, he should respond with a sarcastic tone when he says 'Lady Disdain'.

Benedick should try to provoke Beatrice by boasting 'I am loved of all ladies' as he struts across the stage.

Pick out and comment on words or phrases from the text which show how he should speak and act in Extract 2.

Comment on words and show how he should speak and act in Extract 1. Illustrate by picking out words or phrases from the text.

As a director what advice would you give to an actor playing Benedick on how to respond to Beatrice in these two extracts?

Benedick should use all the anti-female views of the time to put Beatrice down, finally using three words 'disgust', 'horror' and 'perturbation' speaking slowly and drawing out the last word for effect.

In Extract 1 'I love none' should be said with the emphasis on 'I' to show how flippant he is then. He should speak bitterly when he compares her to 'hell' and a 'harpy' in Extract 2.

The actor should show how Benedick changes between Extract 1 and Extract 2. In Extract 1 he is playing word games with Beatrice; in Extract 2 his pride is hurt.

Comment on how the actor could convey Benedick's character on stage.

His joking, light-hearted tone in Extract 1 changes and in Extract 2 he should try to make the lords feel sorry for him. This is very different from the mood of the 'merry war' in Extract 1.

Benedick's arrival, brings humour and joking, but by the time he escapes wounded by 'my Lady Tongue', we realise there are deeper feelings at work.

At first, the actor should focus only on his male friends, until Beatrice gains his attention by insulting him. He responds with bravado and boasting: he declares 'I am loved of all ladies' as he struts across the stage. However, by the second extract he should seem less sure of himself, perhaps conscious that he has let Beatrice down in the past.